ENERGY Revolution

Harnessing Power from the Sun

Niki Walker

 Crabtree Publishing Company
www.crabtreebooks.com

Crabtree Publishing Company

www.crabtreebooks.com

Coordinating editor: Ellen Rodger

Project editor: Carrie Gleason

Editors: Rachel Eagen, Adrianna Morganelli, L. Michelle Nielsen

Production coordinator: Rosie Gowsell

Production assistant: Samara Parent

Art director: Rob MacGregor

Photo research: Allison Napier

Photographs: AP/World Wide Photos: p. 13 (top and bottom), p. 17 (top), p. 21 (middle and bottom left), p. 25 (bottom), p. 28 (top), p. 30; Ajanta, Maharashtra, India, Dinodia/The Bridgeman Art Library: p. 23 (top); David Bathgate/Corbis: p. 16 (top); Corbis: p. 3 (bottom left); Han Dan/epa/Corbis: p. 29 (bottom left); Alberto Estevez/epa/Corbis: cover; Owen Franken/Corbis: p. 25 (top); Waltraud Grubitzsch/epa/Corbis: p. 19 (top); George H. H. Huey/Corbis: p. 22; Danny Lehman/Corbis: p. 1; Reuters/Corbis: p. 5 (top), p. 31 (bottom); Permission for use by ®ENERGY STAR: p. 9 (middle left); Betsy Dupuis/istock International: Rosie the Riveter icon; Mark

Chilvers/Insight/ Panos Pictures: p. 18 (bottom); Penny Tweedie/Panos Pictures: p. 17 (bottom); Mark Boulton/Photo Researchers, Inc.: p. 10 (top); Colin Cuthbert/Photo Researchers, Inc.: p. 20; Georg Gerster/Photo Researchers, Inc.: p. 26; Maximilian Stock Ltd/Photo Researchers, Inc.: p. 27 (bottom); NASA/Photo Researchers, Inc.: p. 31 (top); John Mead/Photo Researchers, Inc.: p. 14 (top); Rosenfeld Images Ltd./Photo Researchers, Inc.: p. 16 (bottom); other images from stock CD.

Illustrations: Rob MacGregor: p. 12, p. 27 (top); Margaret Amy Salter: p. 8

Cover: Giant solar panels stand in Barcelona, Spain.

Title page: This home in sunny New Mexico is an example of how people are building more earth-friendly homes that use the Sun's power directly, and using technology, such as the solar panels shown here, as a source for generating electricity.

Library and Archives Canada Cataloguing in Publication

Walker, Niki, 1972-
        Harnessing power from the sun / Niki Walker.

(Energy revolution)
Includes index.
ISBN-13: 978-0-7787-2912-9 (bound)
ISBN-10: 0-7787-2912-5 (bound)
ISBN-13: 978-0-7787-2926-6 (pbk)
ISBN-10: 0-7787-2926-5 (pbk)

        1. Solar energy--Juvenile literature. I. Title. II. Series.

TJ810.3.W34 2006   j621.47   C2006-902464-2

Library of Congress Cataloging-in-Publication Data

Walker, Niki, 1972-
        Harnessing power from the sun / written by Niki Walker.
        p. cm. -- (Energy revolution)
        Includes index.
        ISBN-13: 978-0-7787-2912-9 (rlb)
        ISBN-10: 0-7787-2912-5 (rlb)
        ISBN-13: 978-0-7787-2926-6 (pbk)
        ISBN-10: 0-7787-2926-5 (pbk)
        1. Solar energy--Juvenile literature. I. Title. II. Series.
        TJ810.3.W35 2006
        621.47--dc22
                                2006014368

Crabtree Publishing Company

www.crabtreebooks.com   1-800-387-7650

Published in Canada
Crabtree Publishing
616 Welland Ave.
St. Catharines, ON
L2M 5V6

Published in the United States
Crabtree Publishing
PMB16A
350 Fifth Ave., Suite 3308
New York, NY 10118

Published in the United Kingdom
Crabtree Publishing
White Cross Mills
High Town, Lancaster
LA1 4XS

Published in Australia
Crabtree Publishing
386 Mt. Alexander Rd.
Ascot Vale (Melbourne)
VIC 3032

Contents

Energy Conservation: 'We Can Do It!'

"We Can Do It" was a slogan that appeared on posters made during World War II. One poster featured "Rosie the Riveter," a woman dressed in blue coveralls (shown below). The poster was originally intended to encourage women to enter the workforce in industry to replace the men who left to serve in the war. Today, the image of Rosie the Riveter represents a time when people came together as a society to reach a common goal. Today's energy challenge can be combatted in a similar way. Together, we can work to save our planet from the pollution caused by burning fossil fuels by learning to conserve energy and developing alternative energy sources.

We Can Do It!

WAR PRODUCTION CO-ORDINATING COMMITTEE

Energy in Our Lives

Without energy, the world would be dark, cold, silent, and completely still. Energy makes things happen. It makes plants and animals live and grow. People also use energy every day to cook food, heat buildings, and run machines.

What is Energy?

Scientists define energy as the **capacity** to do work, or make something happen. There are different forms of energy, such as heat, light, sound, and motion. Energy cannot be created or destroyed, but it can be transferred, or moved from one place to another. For example, when the Sun's rays shine on pavement, some of the Sun's energy is transferred onto the pavement, warming it up. Energy can also be converted, or changed, from one form to another. Special technology, called **solar cells**, can convert the Sun's rays into electricity, or **electrical energy**.

(left) Energy from the Sun is called solar energy. It can be converted into electricity.

(below) Energy is captured and stored in batteries for future use.

Solar energy is used to power these cars. Scientists are working to develop technology that will one day allow full-sized vehicles to run on solar power. Most automobiles currently run on gasoline.

Limited and Limitless

Anything that has energy can be used as an **energy source**. Energy sources include the Sun, wind, moving water, and fossil fuels — coal, oil, and natural gas. There are two types of energy sources: **renewable** and non-renewable. Non-renewable sources cannot be replaced quickly once they are used. Coal, oil, and gas are all non-renewable. Renewable sources are continually replaced, either by people or by nature. Renewable sources are also known as alternative, or "green" energy because they are less harmful to our natural environment. Solar energy is a renewable energy source.

Electricity

Most machines and household appliances are powered by electricity. Electricity is used to store, move, and deliver a form of energy called electrical energy. Electrical energy is often converted from another energy source, such as fossil fuels or moving water. Electricity is measured in watts. The higher its wattage, the more electricity a machine uses. Pictured below are some common household appliances and the power they use:

HAIR DRYER 1,250 watts

OVEN 3,400 watts

CLOTHES DRYER 5,000 watts

Conservation Tip

Energy conservation means reducing the amount of power that we use. You can find tips on how to conserve energy, and facts about energy conservation in boxes like these.

Energy Challenge

Fossil fuels are the most commonly used energy sources around the world today. Coal, oil, and natural gas are fossil fuels. Fossil fuels formed millions of years ago from the remains of plants and animals. Most have to be extracted, or mined, from below ground and **refined** before they are burned for energy.

Fossil Fuel Dependent

Many products are made from fossil fuels. Gasoline, oil, and diesel fuel are fossil fuel products burned for energy in cars and trucks. Natural gas, coal, and oil are fossil fuels that are burned in furnaces for heat. Worldwide, coal is the most used energy source for making electricity in **power plants**. Many of the machines commonly used today are designed to run on fossil fuels. Car engines are built to burn gasoline and truck engines use diesel fuel.

Supply and Demand

As the world population grows, so does the demand for energy. There are only a limited amount of fossil fuels on Earth. Scientists estimate there is less than 100 years' worth of oil and natural gas, and enough coal to last about 250 years. The way we live affects how much energy we use. The United States uses more energy than any other country in the world. It uses more than twice as much energy as China, which has more than four times as many people. The **standard of living** in the United States, as well as in Canada, most areas of Europe, and Australia, is high. People in these countries often live in large homes that require a lot of energy to heat and cool. They drive their own cars and trucks, and consume many goods that require fossil fuel energy to manufacture, sell, and deliver. In order to keep living this way, people must conserve energy, and learn to use alternative energy sources.

(top) **When automobiles burn gasoline for fuel, polluting waste gases, or exhaust, are created.**

(left) **A tower at a coal-fired power plant.**

Global Warming

One of the gases released when fossil fuels are burned is carbon dioxide. Carbon dioxide is a greenhouse gas. Greenhouse gases exist naturally in the Earth's atmosphere. These gases trap heat and light from the Sun and keep it close to Earth. When too much carbon dioxide is produced, from car exhaust and coal-fired power plants, too much heat gets trapped, causing temperatures on Earth to rise. This creates a problem that scientists have named global warming. Scientists believe the long-term effects of global warming will include more severe storms, massive flooding of coastal cities, and even droughts and crop failures in some areas of the world.

(left) As global warming heats up the Earth, the ice that covers the North and South Pole will begin to melt. The melting ice will cause ocean levels to rise and coastal cities to flood.

Conservation Tip

Electricity is used to run air conditioners. The methods we use for producing electricity also create carbon dioxide, which is one of the greenhouse gases that causes high summer temperatures. Keeping curtains closed and turning down air conditioners when you are not home prevents the hot summer Sun from heating up the house, and saves on electricity use!

The Sun's Energy

Energy from the Sun is called solar energy. Solar energy can be used instead of fossil fuels to make electricity. It is also used directly, to provide light and heat, without having to be converted into another form of energy. Solar power does not create pollution or contribute to global warming, and it is a renewable energy source.

Radiating Energy

The Sun is a huge ball of burning gases. Every second, explosions in its core, or center, release enormous amounts of energy. This energy slowly moves from the core to the Sun's surface and then radiates, or travels in **waves**, through space. The energy reaches Earth as heat and light. In just one minute, more solar energy reaches Earth than people use in an entire year!

Energy from Biomass

Many alternative energy sources have their roots in energy gained from the Sun. The Sun's energy helps grow plants than can be turned into fuels called biomass. Biomass fuels can be made from wood, grass, or even cereal crops. Crops, such as corn and sugar, are converted to a **biogas** called ethanol, which is used to fuel cars. When biomass is burned, it releases the energy that the plant has stored. Animal waste and garbage are also made into biomass.

(right) Plants capture and convert sunlight into food during photosynthesis. When animals and people eat the plants, the stored energy is passed along the food chain.

Creating Wind Power

Solar energy also creates wind. Energy from the Sun warms the air and causes it to rise. Cool air moves in to fill the space. This moving air is wind. By harnessing the energy of the wind, electricity can be generated using wind **turbines**. Without the Sun, there would be no wind.

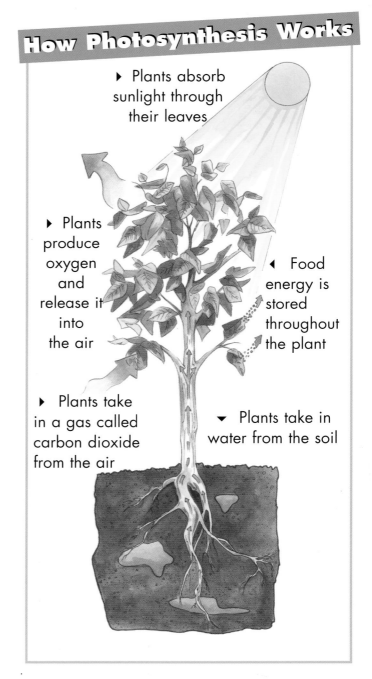

How Photosynthesis Works

▸ Plants absorb sunlight through their leaves

▸ Plants produce oxygen and release it into the air

◂ Food energy is stored throughout the plant

▸ Plants take in a gas called carbon dioxide from the air

▾ Plants take in water from the soil

Sun's Fossil Fuels

Even fossil fuels are a product of the Sun! Fossil fuels are the remains of plants that captured solar energy hundreds of millions of years ago, and of the animals that ate them. When these living things died, they were buried in layers of mud, which kept them from rotting. More mud piled on them, and over time, the **pressure** caused the remains to change. The remains of sea animals became oil and gas, and plants became coal. When fossil fuels are burned, the energy from the Sun captured long ago is released.

(above) Wind is caused by the Sun's energy. On wind farms, turbines capture this energy to make electricity.

Efficiency

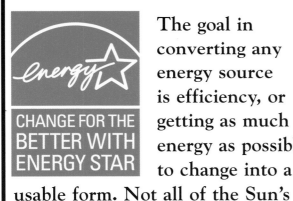

CHANGE FOR THE BETTER WITH ENERGY STAR

The goal in converting any energy source is efficiency, or getting as much energy as possible to change into a usable form. Not all of the Sun's energy that reaches Earth can be changed into electricity. Some of it always changes into a form that is not wanted at that time. Energy efficiency also applies to technology. Many newer household appliances use less energy than older ones that perform the same function, which makes them more energy efficient.

(above) Appliances that have earned the ENERGY STAR are more energy efficient.

Conservation Tip

Make the switch! Regular **incandescent** light bulbs waste a lot of energy by heating up. Switch to compact fluorescent light bulbs - they use less energy to produce the same amount of light.

Let the Sun Shine In

People do not need fancy or expensive equipment to use solar energy. Drying laundry outside on a sunny day is one example of how to use solar energy. By making a few smart choices, people can use the Sun to greatly reduce the need for other energy sources. Using solar energy without extra, specialized equipment is called passive solar energy.

Greenhouse Heat

Passive solar energy can be used for heating buildings. Greenhouses use passive solar energy to create conditions indoors so that plants can grow, even when it is cold outside. Greenhouses are designed to take in and hold the Sun's heat. Glass panels let in sunlight, which warms up the greenhouse, but do not let out the heat.

Conservation Tip

Plan laundry days to take advantage of passive solar energy. By hanging wet laundry on a clothesline to dry, you can save the electricity that it takes to run the clothes dryer.

(above) The Eden Project is an environmental greenhouse project in England. The domes are made from a special type of plastic that allows the Sun's rays in, creating tropical warmth. Tropical plants that cannot usually grow in England, such as banana, rubber, and bamboo trees, thrive inside the domes.

Sunlit Rooms

One of the simplest ways to take advantage of passive solar energy is to let the light in. By opening blinds and curtains, light from the Sun reduces the amount of electric lighting needed in a room. In homes and other buildings, designers put windows high up walls, which lets in extra light. These windows are called **clerestory** windows. Skylights, or windows in the roof, are also built in to provide light to rooms that have no outside walls. The positioning of these windows lets in light but limited heat, so they are commonly used in warm climates.

Solar Cooling

A **thermal** chimney is a **ventilation system** that helps keep a building cool without using air conditioning. Air that has been warmed by the Sun rises, so a thermal chimney has vents high up to let the warm air out. Cooler air is let into a building from lower to the ground on a shaded side of the building. To test how solar cooling works, open a window at the top of the stairs on a hot day. Downstairs, open windows that are low to the ground and are on a shady or northward-facing wall. The warm air will rise up, and out of the building through the open window. Cool air from the downstairs window will replace it. This is called the thermal chimney effect.

Sunny South

In the northern hemisphere, **passive solar buildings face south, toward the equator, where the Sun's rays are strongest. By building homes with large windows in southward-facing walls, these rays enter rooms and heat them.** Overhangs **are built outside the windows to control the amount of Sun that enters a room.**

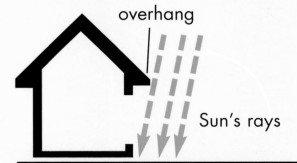

▲ *In summer, the Sun is high in the sky. Overhangs prevent the Sun's rays from entering windows and overheating rooms.*

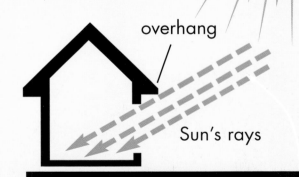

▲ *In winter, the Sun is low in the sky, so the Sun's rays enter windows without interference from overhangs to provide heat.*

Catching the Heat

Using simple devices, people can gather and use more of the Sun's energy. Solar collectors work similar to greenhouses to collect the Sun's energy. Solar collectors absorb, or take in, energy from the Sun, convert it to heat, and transfer it to air or water. Then the heat is piped or fanned to where it is needed. Solar collectors are used to heat buildings and swimming pools, and to heat water for showers, laundry, and other household uses. Larger, more complicated collectors gather enough solar energy to run power plants and produce electricity.

Solar Heated Water

Solar collectors are usually placed on the roofs of buildings, where they receive plenty of direct sunshine. Flat-plate collectors are the most common solar collectors. Most flat-plate collectors are black-lined boxes with glass tops. The Sun shines through the top glass layer of the collector and is absorbed by dark-colored absorber plates. Absorber plates convert the light energy into heat energy. As heat builds up, it is passed on to pipes carrying water. The pipes lead to a storage tank, where hot water is held until it is needed for baths, showers, and washing dishes.

Conservation Tip

In your kitchen at home, the microwave uses less energy than a full-sized oven to do the same job. This makes microwaves more energy efficient.

Solar Space Heating

Solar collectors are also used to warm the air in buildings. Instead of pipes carrying water, the pipes in the collector carry air. The air is pumped into the solar collector from inside the building, warmed, and then fanned back out as hot air.

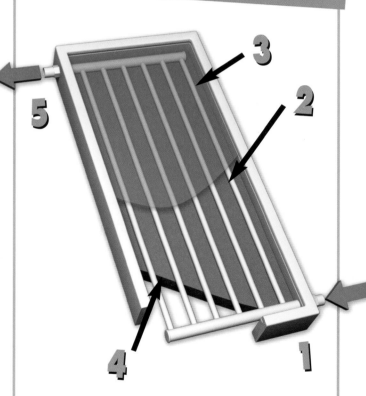

How a Flat-Plate Collector Works

1 Cool water enters the collector.
2 The water fills the pipes.
3 A glass layer allows the sunlight in.
4 A dark-colored absorber plate collects the Sun's energy.
5 The water is warmed and then pumped around a building to where it is needed.

Solar Cookers

Solar cookers are ovens that use solar energy to cook food. Solar cookers have shiny metal surfaces that concentrate solar energy. Concentrating energy means gathering the energy from a wide area and bringing it together in one small spot. This makes the energy much brighter and hotter. Most cookers reach temperatures between 200° F and 300° F (93° C and 149° C). Some can even reach 450° F (232° C)!

A box cooker has a mirrored lid and lining to reflect sunlight onto pots placed inside it. Its dark bottom helps absorb and hold heat inside.

CASE STUDY

Audubon Goes Solar

The Audubon Society is a well-known organization that works to conserve wildlife habitats. In 2004, the earth-friendly organization's center in Los Angeles, California, became the first building in the city to run entirely off solar power. Heating and cooling systems, water pumps, and computer systems in the center are run by solar energy.

(left) On the roof of the L.A. Audubon building, rows of a type of solar collector called vacuum tubes supply hot water.

Solar Power Plants

Solar energy is used to generate electricity in power plants called solar thermal power plants. Large amounts of solar energy have to be collected to make electricity. This is done using concentrating solar power (CSP) systems. There are three main types of CSP systems: troughs, power towers, and dish-engine systems. Each one collects and concentrates sunlight in its own way. Power towers and trough systems are connected to **generating stations**, where electricity is produced using steam turbines. Dish-engine systems are connected to engines that work similar to car engines.

(above) To receive the most sunlight possible, dish-engine systems turn to follow the Sun through the sky.

(below) Trough-system power plants are named for the long, curved mirrors they use to concentrate sunlight.

Conservation Tip

Some energy specialists estimate that as much as a quarter of the energy we use is wasted. You can prevent energy waste by turning off lights, computers, and other electronic equipment when they are not being used.

Solar One and Two

In 1982, the U.S. Department of Energy built the first power tower, named Solar One, in the Mojave Desert in California. Its purpose was to show that power towers could be used to generate a large amount of electricity for a long period of time. Solar One converted solar energy into 10 megawatts (MW) of electricity, which is enough to power about 10,000 homes. It produced power until 1988, when the government ended the test. In 1992, the U.S. government began working with power companies in California to redesign and improve Solar One. They renamed the plant Solar Two and changed the liquid in the tower's container from water to melted salt, which stores heat better. Solar Two was meant to show that a solar plant could store heat and then use it to make electricity when the Sun was not shining. Solar Two operated successfully from 1996 until 1999.

(right) A power tower is a tall tower with a container of liquid at the top. It is surrounded by thousands of mirrors, all aimed at the container. When the liquid in the tower is heated, it is piped to electricity-generating stations to be used as an energy source.

Solar Cells

Solar cells, or photovoltaic (PV) cells, convert sunlight directly into electricity. They have no moving parts and never die out. As long as the Sun shines, solar cells make electricity. Solar cells are made up of two thin layers of a material called **silicon**. Silicon acts as a semiconductor, which means that when the Sun's energy shines on it, a flow of electricity is produced.

(above) A group of solar cells, called a solar panel, is used by this woman in the Himalaya Mountains to power her winter home.

(below) When the Sun shines on a solar cell, an electric current is produced. Unlike solar collectors, solar cells convert sunlight directly into electricity.

More Cells, More Power

A single solar cell does not produce enough electricity to run anything, so solar cells are grouped together. A number of solar cells wired together form a solar panel. Solar panels are often installed on the roofs of buildings to provide some or all of the electricity the buildings use. To provide even more electricity, a number of panels are connected together to form an **array**.

Portable Power

Solar cells do not need power lines to deliver electricity. They can be set up anywhere, no matter how remote. Today, solar panels and arrays are used to power road signs, buoys, radio transmitters, emergency phones, satellites, and space vehicles. They are also a popular way to power cottages and homes that are not connected to the power grid. Some families live off the grid year-round. Their homes have solar panels that are connected to batteries to store electricity for use at night and on cloudy days.

(above) Helios was a solar-powered aircraft developed by the National Aeronautics and Space Administration (NASA), in the United States. Over 62,000 solar cells covered the upper part of the wings to provide power to run the aircraft's engines.

CASE STUDY

Australia's Bushlight

Great parts of Australia have a very dry climate and few people live there. The cost of setting up power lines to the people who do live in these areas is too high. "Bushlight" is a program run by the Australian government that supplies alternative power sources to communities in these remote areas of Australia. Solar panels have been installed to replace the use of diesel generators with a renewable and dependable energy supply. People living there are now able to run refrigerators, televisions, and fans using the Sun's power.

(above) In this remote Australian town, people gather at a resource center to use computers powered by solar panels.

Power Grid

The power grid is the system of power stations, power lines (right), and transformers through which electricity passes to reach your home. Electricity produced by solar thermal power plants also travels the power grid, but power that has been produced by rooftop solar panels does not come from the power grid. In some cases, home solar panels produce enough electricity to power the building on which they are placed, and to sell extra power back to the power grid.

PV Power Plants

Solar arrays are built large enough to supply some or all of the electricity needs of a town or city. These arrays are connected to the power grid, and they are known as PV power plants. PV power plants can be built quickly, and solar panels can be added or taken away, depending on how much electricity is needed. PV power plants send electricity into the power grid just as other power plants do. The electricity that PV power plants produce is called direct current (DC). The type of electricity that comes out of wall sockets in homes is alternating current (AC). A special machine called an inverter is used at power plants to change electricity from DC to AC.

(left) Solar cells are grouped together into a panel to provide enough power to run this telephone booth.

PUBLIC
TELEPHONE هاتف عمومي

The Future of PV

Scientists are working on new technology that will make it easier than ever to use solar energy. Some of these new technologies include PV roof shingles and PV coatings for windows, and are already for sale. Other new developments include rolls of thin, flexible PV and peel-and-stick PV. In the near future, people may peel and stick PV panels to their jackets or backpacks to charge cell phones, laptops, and other devices while they are outdoors. These new PV cells are made of different materials than traditional PV cells. They are less efficient than regular solar cells, but they are also much less expensive.

(above) In June 2005, one of the world's largest PV power plants, began operating in Bavaria, Germany. The power plant is made up of 57,600 solar panels that are arranged in arrays at three different sites. They cover a total area bigger than 50 football fields!

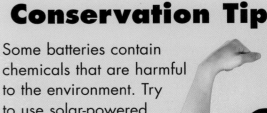

Conservation Tip

Some batteries contain chemicals that are harmful to the environment. Try to use solar-powered devices, such as solar calculators, instead.

19

Smart Solar Designs

Buildings that use solar energy can have a combination of passive solar energy, solar collectors, and solar panels. Homes, businesses, schools, and even farms and factories can be solar-powered. Some new communities now being designed are solar-powered, too.

(below) This office building was designed with solar power in mind. During the day, electricity to run computers, lights, and office equipment comes from the many solar panels covering the front of the building.

Wave of the Future

Competitions take place around the world for the best solar designs. Two of the most famous solar competitions are the North American Solar Challenge and the World Solar Challenge. The North American Solar Challenge gives teams made up of college and university students the chance to build solar-powered cars and race them from Texas, U.S.A. to Alberta, Canada. The World Solar Challenge takes place in Australia. Teams from around the world race their solar-powered cars across the country. There are also solar competitions in home building, in which teams of scientists build homes that are energy efficient. Together, these competitions help raise awareness for renewable energy and develop solar technology.

Earthship Living

Earthship is a passive solar design for buildings made from recycled and natural materials. Originally, these houses were built in the hot, sunny climate of New Mexico, U.S.A. The building designs can also be modified for colder climates. The walls of Earthship buildings are made from old tires and dirt. During the day, the tires absorb heat from the Sun, which they let out at night for heating. To prevent the buildings from overheating in the summer, the southward-facing windows are angled so that direct sunlight does not enter.

(below, right) Earthship designs feature alternative energy sources and natural and recycled building materials. The large windows provide passive solar energy.

(below) The interior of Earthship homes are filled with natural light, which allows for indoor gardening, as in greenhouses.

Conservation Tip

Solar-powered cars are a long way off for future transportation, but you can help reduce the pollution created by cars and trucks by walking, biking, or taking public transportation.

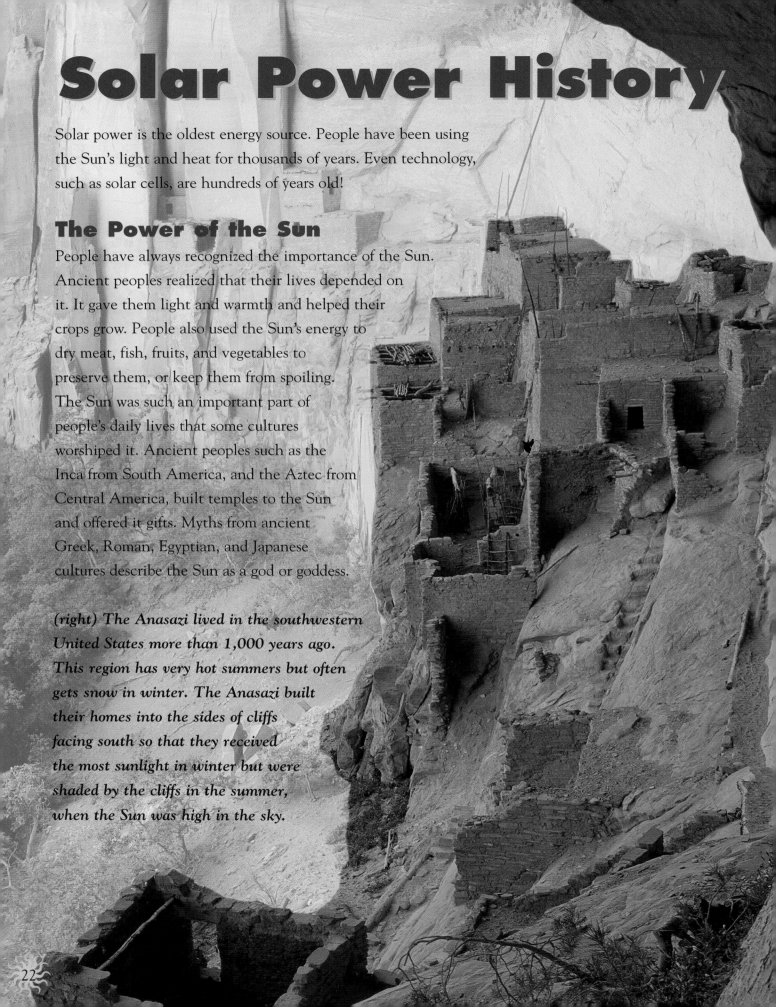

Solar Power History

Solar power is the oldest energy source. People have been using the Sun's light and heat for thousands of years. Even technology, such as solar cells, are hundreds of years old!

The Power of the Sun

People have always recognized the importance of the Sun. Ancient peoples realized that their lives depended on it. It gave them light and warmth and helped their crops grow. People also used the Sun's energy to dry meat, fish, fruits, and vegetables to preserve them, or keep them from spoiling. The Sun was such an important part of people's daily lives that some cultures worshiped it. Ancient peoples such as the Inca from South America, and the Aztec from Central America, built temples to the Sun and offered it gifts. Myths from ancient Greek, Roman, Egyptian, and Japanese cultures describe the Sun as a god or goddess.

(right) The Anasazi lived in the southwestern United States more than 1,000 years ago. This region has very hot summers but often gets snow in winter. The Anasazi built their homes into the sides of cliffs facing south so that they received the most sunlight in winter but were shaded by the cliffs in the summer, when the Sun was high in the sky.

Ancient Solar Homes

Some ancient peoples, such as the Greeks and Romans and the Anasazi of the southwestern United States, used passive solar energy to heat and light their homes. They discovered that by facing their homes to the south, they could capture more of the Sun's warmth in winter. The ancient Greeks even planned entire towns so that each house could receive the most sunlight possible in winter. In ancient Rome, laws were passed to guarantee that people's homes had access to sunlight.

Early Technology

In the 1700s, scientists discovered that they could use mirrors and lenses to focus and concentrate sunlight. In 1700, French scientist Antoine LaVoisier built the first **solar furnace**, a device used to melt metals. Over the next 200 years, scientists and inventors created more devices to harness solar energy. In 1767, Swiss **naturalist** Horace de Saussure built the first solar collector, which was made of glass. The first solar cells were invented in the late 1800s. They were made of different materials than today's cells, and they did not generate much electricity so people did not pay much attention to them. Other solar technology became very popular, however, such as a solar water heater created by American inventor Clarence Kemp in 1891.

Conservation Tip

In the past, people fetched water from an outdoor pump, gathered wood to make a fire, and heated the water over it. Today, hot water comes from our taps, but an energy source is still used to heat it. One way you can conserve hot water is to do laundry using cold instead of hot or warm water.

(above) Many cultures have creation legends that include the Sun. In this Indian legend, the Monkey God is talking to the Sun God.

Firing Up A Revolution

During the 1700s and 1800s, a major change happened in Europe and North America. This change is known as the **Industrial Revolution**. It was a time when people began using machines to do more work. Factories were built, and trains, cars, and planes were invented. People needed more energy than ever to run these new technologies. Coal provided a cheap and easy-to-use energy supply. As a fossil fuel, coal could produce more power than other sources, such as water, wind, or solar power. Very quickly, fossil fuels became the main energy source.

1973 Oil Crisis

During the 1900s, people around the world began using **petroleum products** such as oil and natural gas to run cars and trucks and heat their homes. Oil was also used in industry. Over time, a lot of oil was discovered in the Middle East, such as the countries of present-day Iran, Iraq, Kuwait, and Saudi Arabia. People in the United States and other countries realized the danger of depending on other countries for their main energy source during the oil crisis of 1973. During the crisis, Middle Eastern countries refused to sell them oil. Around the world, the demand for oil was greater than the amount available, and prices rose.

CASE STUDY

Solar Power in Space

The first modern solar cells were made in 1954 by Bell Laboratories, in New Jersey. Around that time, NASA, the American space agency, was searching for a way to power its satellites (**right**). Solar cells were used because they were lightweight, portable, and had no moving parts that would wear out or break in space. In 1958, NASA launched the first solar-powered satellite, *Vanguard I*. Solar cells have played an important part in NASA missions ever since. Today, solar cells still power satellites and other space equipment.

Solar's Rise to Power

As a result of the oil crisis, many governments decided they needed to reduce their countries' dependence on oil and find alternative energy sources. Solar energy was one such source. Governments spent millions of dollars to research and develop better solar technologies. They encouraged families and businesses to buy solar panels and flat-plate collectors by paying part of the cost. Sales of these devices boomed. Then, in the mid-1980s, the price of oil and other fossil fuels dropped. Most people lost interest in solar energy and other alternatives to fossil fuels.

(right) During the 1973 oil crisis, the cost of driving a car shot up overnight and some gas stations ran out of gas to sell.

(below) In the late 1970s, new communities were planned and built to take advantage of passive solar designs and new solar technology.

Solar Power Limits

In the past ten years, scientists have improved solar technology, making it easier to use, more affordable, and more efficient. Despite all of the benefits of solar power, there are still some drawbacks.

Weather Permitting

In most parts of the world, solar energy is an **intermittent** energy source, which means that it is not available all the time. Less solar energy is available on cloudy days and in winter, and at night it is not available at all. Storing solar energy in batteries can help make it a more reliable source, but the batteries are large, expensive, and need to be maintained.

Efficiency

The Earth receives an enormous amount of energy from the Sun every second. This energy is difficult to harness because much of it is spread out over the entire surface of the planet. Solar technology cannot convert all of the solar energy it receives into electricity. Scientists are constantly improving the efficiency of solar technology. For example, solar cells in the 1970s converted only about six percent of solar energy into electricity. Today's cells can convert more than 20 percent.

(below) Solar power plants take up huge amounts of space in deserts.

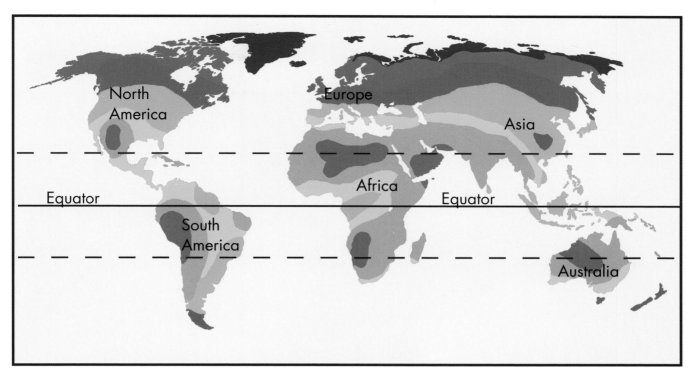

Cost Concerns

The Sun's energy reaches Earth for free, but the technology needed to harness that power is still very expensive. In areas with inexpensive electricity produced by other energy sources, installing solar panels may not pay off. Solar panels are costly because the silicon used to make them is expensive. Silicon is also used to make computer parts, so there is high demand for it. Solar cells are also made by hand, and not yet mass-produced in factories, which makes them more expensive. Mass production makes goods less expensive — the more goods a factory can produce, the less expensive each one becomes to make. Solar cells could become less expensive if more people bought them, but most people will not buy them until their price comes down.

(right) This factory worker is making solar cells, which are joined together to make the solar panels behind her.

(above) The areas shaded red on the map receive the most solar energy, blue shows the least. Some parts of the world are well-suited to solar power plants because they receive a strong, steady supply of sunlight almost every day of the year.

Making the Change

Solar energy is set to replace some of the fossil fuels people use today. Using solar energy reduces the damage people are doing to the environment by burning fossil fuels. Making the switch to solar energy takes time, money, and planning. More solar power plants will need to be built and millions of solar panels installed on rooftops.

Getting a Break

In some parts of the world, there are government incentives to use solar power. This means that governments encourage people and businesses to install solar panels and solar water heaters by reducing the amount of taxes they pay and offering **rebates** for part of the cost.

Conservation Tip

Try not to buy things you do not really need. Everything you buy takes energy to manufacture and get to the store. When you are finished with toys, and other items, pass them along to someone else who can use them.

(above) Some state governments in the United States have "million solar roofs" programs. The state pays part of the cost of buying and installing solar panels. They hope to have solar panels on a million roofs within a certain length of time.

Everyone's Doing It!

Individuals can make the biggest difference when it comes to switching energy sources. By buying and using solar technology, people support solar energy businesses while reducing the amount of fossil fuels they use. People can also install PV windows, roof shingles, solar water heaters, and solar panels on their homes. Extra electricity can be sold back into the grid, which helps reduce the amount of electricity that has to be produced by power plants that burn fossil fuels. People can also choose to build passive solar homes. These homes cost no more to build than others. Finally, one of the most important things people can do is to learn more about solar energy and solar technology, and spread the word!

People think of ingenious ways to use solar power, such as this solar-powered vehicle.

Role Models

In recent years, Germany and Japan have become world leaders in using solar energy. One of the main reasons solar energy is so popular in these countries is that their governments have helped make it competitive with the cost of fossil fuels. Fossil fuels are more expensive in Germany and Japan than they are in North America. Governments there pay part of the cost of buying solar panels, and they insist that power companies buy the extra electricity the panels produce. People have installed hundreds of thousands of panels as a result, which has greatly increased the amount of electricity produced from solar energy.

Solar cells can be attached to almost anything to harness the Sun's energy.

Timeline

For millions of years, people's energy needs were simple. Animals, moving water, the Sun, and the wind were used as energy sources. As people's lives changed through the use of machines, electricity, and transportation, their energy needs grew and changed. Most of this energy now comes from fossil fuels, but in order to create a future with reliable, affordable, and clean energy, people will have to rely increasingly on alternative energy sources, such as solar power. Here is a list of some important milestones in the development of solar technology.

This offshore fish feeding tank is powered by solar and wind energy.

1839

French scientist Edmond Becquerel discovers the photovoltaic effect, which is the production of electricity when light hits certain materials. His discovery will later be the basis of solar cells.

1876

The first solar cells are created. They do not produce enough electricity to power electrical devices, but prove for the first time that electricity does not have to be made using heat or machines.

1891

Clarence Kemp **patents** the first solar water heater. Before his invention, people heated water on stoves or put water in black tanks outside. Heating water in these tanks took many hours, and the water did not remain warm for long.

1909

Solar water heaters that are similar to the flat-plate collectors of today are invented. The heated water is stored in a tank indoors, so it does not cool off overnight.

1954

Bell Laboratories create the first photovoltaic cell that is powerful enough to run electronic equipment.

1981

Stephen R. Ptacek flies a solar-powered airplane, the *Solar Challenger*, across the English Channel, between England and France. The plane is powered by 16,128 solar cells.

1982

Hans Tholstrup builds and drives the first solar-powered car, called the *Quiet Achiever*, more than 2,515 miles (4,058 km) across Australia. That same year, Solar One, the world's largest solar power station, begins operating in California as a demonstration of solar energy's abilities.

1987

Hans Tholstrup's solar-powered car trip in 1982 inspires him to start a solar-powered car race, known as the World Solar Challenge. The race has been held every year since.

1993

Pacific Gas & Electric in California builds the first PV power plant connected to the power grid.

1996

Solar One is redesigned and renamed Solar Two. It is meant to test the possibility of storing solar energy, and proves that it can be done.

1998

American scientist Subhendu Guha invents solar shingles, which allow a roof to turn solar energy into electricity.

2005

Solar cell efficiency improves so that 40 percent of the Sun's energy that hits each cell can be converted into electricity.

(above) The Gossamer Penguin, *a solar-powered plane, on a 1979 test flight.*

(below) A boy shows the solar cell that powers his toy.

Glossary

array A grouping of arranged objects

atmosphere The layers of gases surrounding Earth

biogas A gas that can be used as fuel. It is formed by rotting organic, or once living, matter

capacity The amount that can be performed or produced

clerestory Windows in the uppermost part of a wall

diesel generator A machine that burns diesel fuel to create power

electrical energy A type of energy created by electrical charges

energy source Anything that has or contains energy and can be used to make power

generating station A place where electricity is produced

incandescent Something that gets so hot that it glows light

Industrial Revolution A period in history when machines were invented and factories opened, leading to a change in the way people lived

intermittent Starting and stopping at regular periods of time

naturalist A person who studies plants and animals in nature

northern hemisphere The part of Earth north of the Equator

overhang Part of the roof that protrudes, or hangs over, a wall

patent A special license that recognizes and gives rights to the inventor of something

petroleum products Products such as gasoline, plastics, natural gas, and parafin wax that are refined from petroleum or oil

power plant A place where electricity is produced; a generating station

pressure The weight of something pushing down on another object

rebate Money given back to someone for purchasing a product

refine To change something to make it purer

renewable Able to be replaced

satellite An object in space that orbits a planet

silicon An element that occurs naturally on Earth

solar cell A device made from silicon that produces an electric current when the Sun shines on it

solar furnace A metal box that concentrates solar energy

standard of living The way that people in a certain place live

thermal Temperature or heat; a rising column of warm air

transformer A device that changes an electrical current

turbine A machine with blades that spin and are attached to a shaft

ventilation system A series of passages that allow fresh air exchange in a building

wave A type of movement that goes up and down or back and forth

Index

Printed in the U.S.A.